How Animals Behave

Animal Defenses

Jeremy Cherfas

V

Lerner Publications Company
Minneapolis

Contents

Introduction

Imagine a fox trying to eat a hedgehog, or a cheetah sprinting after a gazelle. The **predator,** the fox or the cheetah, tries its best to catch the **prey,** the hedgehog or gazelle. At the same time, the hedgehog or the gazelle tries its best to keep from being eaten. The hedgehog rolls up into a ball and keeps the fox away with its needle-sharp spines. The gazelle twists and turns and tries to tire the cheetah. In each case, the prey is defending itself against the predator, and usually the prey wins. Cheetahs lose the race four out of five times, and very few hedgehogs are eaten by foxes.

The prey usually wins because it has more at stake. If the cheetah misses, it stays hungry a little longer. If the gazelle does not get away, it dies. Gazelles that are not fast and agile enough to escape a cheetah are quickly weeded out.

To survive, most animals need to keep from being eaten (although we will meet a few in the next chapter that have to be eaten in order to survive). Defenses help to keep an animal alive. In this book, we will look at some of the ways that animals defend themselves.

The Australian echidna, or spiny anteater, has sharp spines as a defense against enemies. Echidnas also defend themselves by burrowing in the ground, as the one in the picture is doing.

A cheetah chasing a zebra on the plains of East Africa. Like gazelles, zebras are slower than cheetahs but can keep running for a longer time.

1 / Staying Alive

Animals must eat to live. Some eat plants, some eat other animals, and some eat both, but all need food. In order to stay alive, most animals also need to keep from being eaten by anything else. But there are a few animals that actually need to be eaten in order to live.

Parasites are living things that take food directly from another larger living thing, their **host**. In doing so, they often harm it. The fleas that live on my cat are parasites. The cat is their host. Other parasites live inside their hosts and during some part of their lives may have to move from one host to another. They do that by being eaten.

There is a kind of parasitic worm that spends the first part of its life in a small shrimp-like animal, and the rest in mallard ducks. When the parasites are ready to change hosts, they make the shrimp behave oddly. Normally, the shrimp avoids light and stays near the bottom of the pond. But when a shrimp is infested with parasites, it leaves the bottom and swims up to the surface, where hungry mallards can find and eat it. The parasites get eaten too and complete their life cycle inside the duck.

Unlike these parasites, most animals must protect themselves from being eaten. They may have sharp

A cat flea, seen greatly magnified, hiding in a cat's fur. Less than a tenth of an inch (2 millimeters) long, the flea sucks the cat's blood for food.

Parasites are small animals that live in or on other animals and feed on them. This diagram shows the life cycle of a parasitic worm that spends part of its life inside freshwater shrimp and part inside the ducks that eat the shrimp.

A pill woodlouse rolls itself into a tight ball for protection. This tiny animal, a land-dwelling relative of the shrimp and crab, is covered with hard, overlapping plates.

spines. They may disguise themselves or hide. They may even fight back. You can probably think of many other kinds of defenses.

Any kind of defense usually increases an animal's chances of survival. Animals with good defenses are more likely to survive and reproduce. Their offspring will usually inherit the means of defense that kept the parents alive. At the same time, predators must be able to overcome the defenses of their prey and eat them often enough to stay alive and produce young.

Freshwater shrimp are found in most ponds and lakes. One species of freshwater shrimp often becomes a host to a kind of parasitic worm. It then swims to the surface of the lake and is gobbled up by ducks.

2 / Hide and Seek

One of the simplest ways of staying safe is to hide. Many animals defend themselves in this way. Even an animal as defenseless as an earthworm can find protection within its burrow. A worm digs a burrow by making its front end long and thin and poking it between crumbs of soil. Then it contracts muscles that make its body short and fat. This action pushes against the soil, making firm walls for the burrow.

Earthworms stay in their burrows during the day, but they come up at night, looking for leaves that they pull down into their burrows to eat. Even then, they leave their tails in the burrow so that they can retreat at the first sign of danger. When a bird catches an earthworm above ground, it tugs on the worm, trying to pull it out of the burrow.

Many animals that come out at night spend the day in a hole or burrow. One that almost never comes up is the mole. It spends nearly all its time underground, eating the insects and earthworms that it comes across while digging or that accidentally break through and fall into its tunnels. So hiding underground doesn't always protect the earthworm.

A European song thrush tugging at an earthworm caught above ground during daylight hours

This song thrush is cracking open a snail on a stone. Each bird has its favorite stone, which scientists call an anvil.

Armor

Even simpler, perhaps, than digging a hole is wearing armor plating on your body. Snails and other **mollusks** are good examples of animals that rely on strong armor. Snails have one shell into which they can retreat. Their relatives the **bivalve** mollusks have two shells that shut together. (Mussels and oysters are bivalves.)

Shells are good protection against most predators, but there are some that have found a way through the armor. Birds like the European song thrush smash snails against a stone to crack their shells. Some kinds of sea snails, such as the oyster drill, can scrape a hole through even a thick oyster shell with their hard, rough tongues to get at the soft animal hidden inside.

As you can see, no defense is perfect. If one **species** of animal develops a better defense, such as a thicker shell, sooner or later some other animals develop a way to overcome it. Life is like a constant arms race, with no lasting victory for either side.

Snails move too slowly to escape from enemies. Their shells protect them from many predators, but not from hungry birds.

Camouflage

Some animals are hard to find even when they are out in the open. They blend into the background because they look similar to their surroundings. This is called **camouflage**. One of the experts at camouflage is the ptarmigan, a relative of the grouse that lives in northern regions of Europe and North America.

In summer, you can almost step on a ptarmigan before you see it, so well do its patchy brown feathers hide it in the dry vegetation. In winter, when the ground is covered with snow, the same brown feathers would stick out like a sore thumb. So the ptarmigan, like many other animals, changes color. It becomes almost completely white.

The ptarmigan is a kind of grouse that lives in Canada and Northern Europe. Its plumage changes color with the seasons so that it stays well camouflaged at all times.

Chameleons, like this one in northern Kenya, can change the color of their skin to blend in with almost any surroundings. The chameleon's camouflage hides it both from predators and from the insects it catches with its long tongue.

The ptarmigan takes a few weeks to molt its feathers and change color, but other animals can change much more quickly. You may have heard of the lizard known as the chameleon, which can alter its color and pattern to blend in with its background. Other animals can do the same trick. Flatfish like the flounder match whatever they are resting on, whether it is sand, pebbles, or a checkerboard put out by a scientist.

Camouflage is important for predators too. A tiger's stripes blend in with the light and shadow of the grasses and trees around it and make it hard to see as it creeps up on its prey.

The plaice is a European flat-fish that spends most of its time on the ocean floor. It can change its color and pattern to match the sand and pebbles under it.

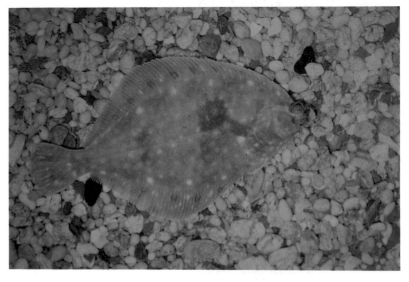

Disguise

What is the difference between camouflage and disguise? One difference might be that a camouflaged animal looks like its surroundings, while a disguised one resembles some other object.

Take stick insects, for example. They look exactly like the branches that they rest on, and they even sway convincingly in the breeze. It is hard to say whether we should call this disguise or camouflage. Whatever we choose to call it, it is clear that many animals go to extraordinary lengths to look like something they are not.

Insects are experts at this kind of disguise. There are insects that look like leaves, some green and alive, others brown and withered. Some insects look like thorns, and some are exactly like small pebbles or stones. But insects are not the only animals that go in for this kind of deception.

This South American stick insect is difficult to spot in its disguise as a twig.

This leaf insect from Costa Rica looks exactly like an old dead leaf. Few birds would recognize it as a possible meal.

The sargassum fish lives among the sargassum weed floating on the surface of many tropical seas. It looks so much like the weed that it is almost completely hidden from predators. The eyes of the fish in this photograph may help you to find it.

Many kinds of fish look very much like dead leaves. One, which lives in the Caribbean, can even change color to match the mangrove leaves floating around it in the water. Some snakes are long and thin and green, and they could easily be mistaken for a vine growing through the bushes. There is even a frog that looks exactly like a bird dropping. It sits out on a leaf, quite exposed, and predators pay no attention to it.

Usually, a disguise like this works well as a defense. But there is a problem. What if a predator learns to watch for things that look like bird droppings? It can become good at telling the real thing from the fakes, and the frogs will not be protected anymore. This sort of thing can happen.

Animals that use disguise usually are not found in large numbers. Because of this, predators don't see enough of them to learn to tell them from the real thing. If there were too many animals using exactly the same disguise, the trick wouldn't work quite so well.

3 / Be Alert

One of the best ways to avoid danger is to be on the lookout. An animal that keeps a careful watch can often see an approaching enemy in time to hide or run away. This is not always practical, however. An animal watching for predators usually isn't able to do other vital things, for example, eating. To solve this problem, many animals come together in groups.

A flock of birds feeding on the lawn is like an animal with eyes in the back of its head. While most of the birds are feeding, one or two will be looking for danger. If they see something alarming and fly away, the whole flock joins them and escapes.

The birds in a flock don't actually take turns watching; it is just that when there are many birds, one or two are always on the alert. The more birds there are in a flock, the more time each of them can spend feeding, without being in any more danger.

A meerkat watching for danger. These small animals from Africa post sentries to guard their nests.

Most members of this flock of brant geese are feeding with heads down, but a few are on the alert for danger. These small geese spend summers in the Arctic and winters in coastal areas in Europe and North America.

Safety in numbers

There may be another good reason to be in a group: it confuses predators. Imagine a single herring swimming along. It would be easy for a predator, a tuna perhaps, to chase it down and swallow it. Now imagine a huge school of thousands of herring, each shining with bright flashes of silver as it swims. It is much harder for the predator to keep an eye on one particular fish. When the fish in the school see a predator chasing them, they twist and turn even more, making it harder still.

Although a large school may be easier for the predator to find, the size also makes it harder for the predator to pick off one particular fish. In a large school, each fish has a greater chance of survival. There is safety in numbers.

Predators might be confused by the large numbers of fusilier fish in this school photographed near the island of Fiji in the South Pacific. For the fish, there is safety in numbers.

Sentries

Flocks of birds and schools of fish do not have actual sentries that watch for danger. Every animal just happens to be alert some of the time. But in some species, animals do take turns performing sentry duty. This is true among meerkats.

Meerkats are small animals related to mongooses. They live in family groups of 12 or more in southern Africa, and their homes are often dug in abandoned termite nests. When meerkats come up out of their burrows, one or two will stand guard. They climb to the top of the termite nests and often stretch up on their back legs to get a better view of their surroundings.

If the sentries see something—for example, an eagle high up in the sky—they give a sharp alarm call. All the meerkats stop what they are doing and keep their eyes on the eagle. If it flies away, they will go back to their activities: feeding, playing, grooming, or whatever. But if the eagle threatens to come close enough to make a pounce on one of the group, all the meerkats will dash down into the safety of their burrows.

After a while, the sentries may get tired. Or perhaps they are hungry or want to join in the games. They make a special noise, and another member of the pack will come and relieve them.

Meerkats keep watch over their den in Namibia, Africa. These little animals live in groups of 12 or more. Normally, only 1 or 2 would be on guard duty, but the meerkats in this picture are all on the alert because they are watching the photographer.

"You can't catch me"

Springboks also use a warning system to avoid predators. Like meerkats, these small antelopes live in southern Africa. They are called springboks because they spring into the air like living pogo sticks. A springbok leaps up, arching its back and putting its head down like a bucking bronco. This is called pronking, and many deer and antelopes do it.

The sight of a springbok pronking like this is a sure sign that there is a predator, usually a lion or cheetah, nearby. Pronking warns the other springboks in the herd, who often start to pronk themselves. It also sends a message to the predator. A predator that has lost the element of surprise cannot hope to catch these fast runners, so it may as well give up and hunt somewhere else.

A springbok in Africa's Kalahari desert pronking to warn other springbok of a predator. A pronking leap may reach 10 feet or more (3 or more meters) in height, and a springbok may pronk five or six times in succession.

An angry mob

Sometimes it is difficult to tell what is the most important form of defense for a group of animals. For example, small birds like sparrows gather in large flocks in the winter. A flock has many eyes on the lookout for danger. That makes it easier for all the birds to escape.

If a predator does attack, it will be confused by the number of targets. Often, a bird of prey like a hawk will try to split one sparrow off from the flock so that it can concentrate its attack.

When they see a hawk or an owl resting in a tree, the little birds often go on the attack themselves. They form an angry mob, diving at the bigger bird's head and pulling at its feathers. If they keep it up, the bird of prey will tire of this harassment and flap off in search of a quieter spot. By being alert, confusing, and angry, the sparrows have successfully defended themselves.

An eagle being mobbed by a group of crows

This marsh hawk, a large American bird of prey, is under attack by a much smaller red-winged blackbird.

4 / *Fight Back*

Sometimes it is hard to know when defense ends and attack begins. Many animals have spines to defend themselves and, like the hedgehog, may roll up in a ball so that all a predator sees is the spines. Porcupines, which also have spines, turn the tables on any animal foolish enough to attack them.

Porcupines live in North and South America, as well as in Africa and Asia, and most kinds defend themselves in the same way. A porcupine will walk backward toward a predator, shaking and rattling its **quills**. If the predator persists in its attack, the porcupine rushes back suddenly and sticks its quills into the animal's face. The quills are loosely attached to the porcupine and come off, remaining stuck in the predator. They also have small **barbs**, which stop the quill from coming out. The wounds made by the quills often become infected, and even animals as big and fierce as leopards and tigers have been found dead with hundreds of porcupine quills stuck in them.

An East African crested porcupine displaying its quills

Poisons

Sometimes spines alone are not enough. Many animals have spines that are equipped with poison. The scorpion fish, which is named after another poisonous animal, is just one of several species of fish that have sacs of poison at the base of the long spines in their fins. If a predator threatens it, the scorpion fish first displays its gaudily colored fins. This is a warning not to go any further.

If the predator does attack, the scorpion fish maneuvers to pierce the attacker with its spines. The pain of the poison is intense, and most predators quickly flee. One that does not is the octopus. For reasons nobody understands, the poison has no effect on the octopus. When an octopus approaches, instead of displaying boldly, the scorpion fish turns tail and flees.

Scorpion fish have sharp, poisonous spines that can inflict very painful wounds on an attacker. Several different kinds of scorpion fish are found in the oceans of the world.

The scorpion fish does not use its poison spines to attack other animals or to catch its own food. They are only defensive. Quite often, however, poison is used for both attack and defense. Venomous snakes, for example, use poison to kill their food. Usually they escape from predators themselves by silently slithering off. But if there is no escape, they will also use their poison to defend themselves.

The bombardier beetle

Nasty chemicals are a very common defense. One of the strangest chemical weapons belongs to the bombardier beetle. These beetles are found all over the world, but are especially common in South America. When a bombardier beetle is attacked, usually by ants, it sprays a boiling hot liquid from the tip of its abdomen. That quickly gets rid of the ants.

The bombardier beetle is like a living chemistry set. In its abdomen it has two compartments, which contain chemicals that are perfectly safe on their own. But when they are mixed, there is a violent chemical reaction that produces heat and gas. The gas blows the mixture out, and the beetle can swivel its abdomen to aim the jet of boiling liquid at whatever has disturbed it.

To defend itself, a bombardier beetle squirts a boiling hot spray of liquid from the end of its abdomen. Substances are combined inside the beetle's body to produce a violent chemical reaction that forces the spray out. A few squirts of this burning liquid will quickly drive away a predator like this frog.

A large sea anemone attacking a grouper fish in the Coral Sea, off the coast of Australia. The anemone's tentacles are covered with stinging cells that inject a poison.

Borrowed weapons

Most animals have their own weapons, but a few borrow them from other species. Some sea slugs borrow stings, and some butterflies borrow poisons.

Sea slugs are related to snails but do not have shells. You might think that this would make them defenseless, but it does not. Even hungry fish avoid eating sea slugs, and one reason is that many of them have stinging cells that can inject the fish with poison. A sea slug gets its defenses by feeding on sea anemones.

This sea slug, photographed near the island of Mauritius in the Indian Ocean, is defending itself by ejecting sticky white strings. Many sea slugs use poison to keep predators away.

Sea anemones, animals related to corals and jellyfish, have wavy tentacles that are covered with stinging cells. Anemones use these cells to capture food and to defend themselves against predators. When anything touches a stinging cell, it shoots out a spine that pierces whatever triggered it and injects a poison.

Stinging cells protect the sea anemone from most predators, but not quite all. Many kinds of sea slugs somehow manage to eat the tentacles without triggering the stinging cells. Once inside the sea slug's body, the stinging cells move to bumps on the animal's back that are something like tentacles. And there they protect the sea slug from predators, just as they protected their former owner the sea anemone.

Another borrowed weapon is the bad taste of the

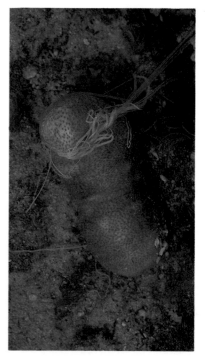

In addition to their stinging cells, anemones have other means of defending themselves. When an anemone is disturbed, it can fold its tentacles inward, as shown in these drawings. The photograph pictures a beadlet anemone, which is found in most parts of the world.

monarch butterfly. Birds, for example, blue jays, like to eat butterflies. The first time a blue jay sees a monarch, it will catch and eat it. But the monarch contains chemicals that make the blue jay sick. It may even vomit. From then on, it will never eat a monarch butterfly.

Monarchs normally lay their eggs on plants called milkweeds, which contain poisons. Most animals avoid the milkweed, but monarch caterpillars can cope with the poison. In fact, a caterpillar feeds on the milkweed leaves and stores the poison in its body. When it has changed into an adult butterfly, the poison eaten by the caterpillar protects the butterfly. If the monarch caterpillars feed on cabbages instead of milkweed, the adult butterflies do not taste bad and blue jays will eat them quite happily.

5 / *Deception*

Monarchs are protected by the poisons they pick up from milkweeds, but birds still have to learn to leave them alone. The butterflies make it easier for the birds by having a bright pattern that is easy to recognize. This is called warning coloration, and it is very common. Animals that are well protected often send out a signal that it is best to leave them alone. The skunk, sauntering along in its bright black and white coat, advertises its ability to spray a very nasty smell. The poisonous rattlesnake buzzes a warning to prevent anybody from coming closer.

These warnings make sense because if a predator learns to avoid such animals, it runs less risk of being harmed. And the prey, giving out the signal, may avoid being injured. But some animals that send out warning signals actually have no protection.

Monarchs and viceroys

A viceroy is someone who takes the place of the monarch, like the Viceroy of India in the old days of the British Empire. That is why the name viceroy is used for another kind of butterfly that looks very much like the monarch. The differences between them are so slight that even a sharp-eyed bird is fooled. A jay that has tasted monarchs will leave viceroys alone too, even though viceroys do not contain poison.

The skunk raises its black-and-white tail as a warning. Any animal that attacks despite the warning will be squirted with a very nasty-smelling spray.

The monarch butterfly (left) and the viceroy (right) look very similar, but only the monarch is poisonous to birds.

This form of defense is called **mimicry**. Of course, the frog we met on page 9 is mimicking a bird dropping, but usually mimicry means copying another animal that has its own protection, rather than merely being disguised.

One mimic that fools many people is the hoverfly, found in almost every garden. Hoverflies have black and yellow stripes, and at first glance they look just like bees or wasps. Look closer, and you can see that the eyes, the wings, and the head are really quite different. But it is that first glance that protects the hoverfly from hungry birds.

This kind of mimicry is very common. For example, there are harmless snakes with the same color pattern as poisonous ones. There are grasshoppers that mimic bombardier beetles and spiders that look like ants. In Borneo, there are five species of tree shrew that taste awful and five species of squirrel that taste good but look so much like the tree shrews that it takes an expert to tell them apart. In all of these cases, the mimic is harmless, but it copies a species that is not.

A hoverfly collecting nectar from a mint flower. These flies look much like bees and wasps but have no stings. They are found in many parts of the world.

Fooling your enemies

The little hog-nosed snake, found throughout most of the United States, is totally harmless. When approached by something large and threatening, it lies perfectly still, relying on its camouflage. But if the threat comes closer, the snake begins to writhe and hiss alarmingly, and may even pretend to strike at the attacker like a poisonous snake. Attackers are usually so startled that they back off and give the snake a chance to escape. If even this trick doesn't work, the hog-nosed snake lies still and pretends to be dead. Predators often lose interest in an animal that appears dead.

These two brightly colored snakes from Costa Rica are difficult to tell apart. But the one in the lower picture is a deadly coral snake, while the other is a harmless mimic. It is safer for predators to avoid both of them.

This plover is trying to keep a warthog away from its nest in the grasslands of Africa. To draw the warthog away, it is pretending to be injured by flapping one wing.

Birds do not often have complicated defenses because they can simply fly away from danger. But what about young chicks, who cannot yet escape? Quite often they are well camouflaged, and at the first sign of danger they freeze, making it very hard to spot them. Even that, however, may not be enough, and so in some species the parent bird goes through an elaborate bit of acting.

When a fox comes close to a killdeer hidden on its nest, the parent bird will sneak quietly away from the eggs or chicks. Then it pops up and attracts the fox's attention. It walks away from the nest, crying piteously and fluttering one wing and dragging it on the ground. The fox certainly seems fooled by all this, because it stalks off after the bird. But when it has led the fox away from the nest, the killdeer leaps up into the air, its "broken" wing miraculously healed, and flies back to its young. It settles down quickly, relying on camouflage to protect it until another fox comes too close.

Heads or Tails?

There are some animals who use their tails to distract predators from the rest of their bodies. The stump-tailed skink, a lizard that lives in Australia, has a short, stumpy tail just as its name says. Its tail looks so much like its head that predators have a hard time deciding which end to attack. If they peck at the tail, the skink has a chance to run down its burrow. Some snakes, such as the burrowing python, raise their tails and move them like a head looking around to make the illusion more convincing.

Some lizards go even further in their attempts to distract a predator. They shed their tails completely. The tail is designed to break off, and continues twitching and wriggling for a while all by itself. The lizard runs off while the predator is watching the tail. In time the lizard will grow a new tail.

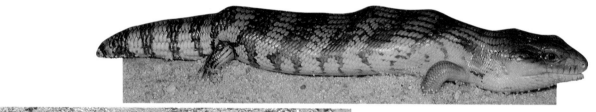

The blue-tongued skink (above) and the stump-tailed skink (below), two Australian lizards, both have short, sturdy tails that look very much like their heads.

6 / Fighting and Defense

Most of this book has described the ways in which animals defend themselves from predators that want to eat them. The predator and its prey almost always belong to different species of animals. But there is another kind of defense, the kind an animal might use when it fights with one of its own species. It could be a dispute about food, or about a **territory**, or about mating. But these fights do not happen because one animal wants to eat the other.

In any fight, there is a good chance that the loser may be severely wounded or even killed. The winner may be injured too and unable to defend itself against a predator. If two animals can settle their dispute without actually fighting, both are usually better off.

Fighting by the rules

One of the simplest ways to settle a dispute over ownership is to obey a rule, such as "finders keepers." Some animals do obey that particular rule. The speckled wood butterfly lives in English woodlands, and in spring the males occupy territories. These territories are the patches of sunlight that filter down through the leaves onto the forest floor. The male sits there, waiting for a female to arrive. When one does, they may fly up into the leaves to mate.

A dispute between a male and female fox. This kind of aggressive behavior between animals of the same species does not often turn into a real fight.

A female (left) and male (right) speckled wood butterfly. In spring, the male establishes a territory in a patch of sunlight in the woodlands.

If it is another male instead of a female who lands in the patch of sunlight, the two males fly spiralling up into the treetop. Then one butterfly leaves, and the other returns to the patch. The odd thing is, it is always the one that was there first that remains. It does not matter how big the intruder is, or how fast he flies, or anything. He always loses. The original finder of a patch always keeps it.

In fact, the dispute between the two speckled wood butterflies is hardly a fight at all. It seems instead to be a mistake, quickly sorted out. The resident stays and the intruder retreats because they both obey the same rule. The only time there is anything approaching a real battle is when two males settle at each end of a particularly large patch of sunlight. Each thinks he is the resident, and when they do finally meet, each expects the other one to retreat. These fluttering fights can go on for several minutes.

The last resort

Not all animals obey rules as simple as the speckled wood butterfly's, but for most of them an actual fight is usually the last resort. Before they decide to fight, they have all sorts of ways to size each other up very carefully. If one is clearly stronger, the weaker animal may give up without a fight.

Brown bears wrestle with each other in the icy waters of Alaska.

Two male red kangaroos fighting. One of these animals will probably give in rather than risk serious injury.

With their antlers locked, two red deer stags fight in head-to-head combat. The winner will gain control of a herd of females.

Red deer, found in Europe, are a perfect example. In the mating season, each **stag** (male deer) tries to keep control over a herd of **hinds** (female deer). He roars out across the glens to advertise his presence. Another stag, who might be thinking of challenging the first stag for his herd, will begin roaring too. The first stag, hearing this, will roar back.

Stags have to put a great deal of effort into roaring, so the stronger a stag is, the faster he can roar. If one stag can roar more often, he is probably stronger and would win a fight. The challenger's best defense is not to attack.

Close combat

If their roaring is similar, the animals may come closer together. They walk up and down, next to one another. Each is checking the other one out, seeing how big he is, how large his antlers are, and whether he looks like a good fighter. Again, the challenger will proceed only if he thinks he stands a good chance of winning.

The antlers of a male red deer are signs of his power and strength. Red deer live in Europe and Asia. They are familiar animals in the highlands of Scotland.

Usually the challenger withdraws, but occasionally he decides to risk a fight. The stags rush at one another, and the mountains echo to the crashing of their antlers. They lock antlers together and push and shove like wrestlers. This fight is still mostly a contest of strength, not a serious attempt to hurt each other. Still, injuries often do occur. Eventually, one animal gives up and runs away. The winner may enjoy his control of the females for a while, but another challenge is sure to come.

Stags do everything they can to avoid a real fight, and this is true of most animals. Very few attack without reason. They do so only when they are hungry or feel threatened themselves.

In this book, we have explored many of the defenses animals use against predators in order to avoid being eaten. When there is a dispute between members of the same species, the rules are different. The best defense then is to avoid a fight unless you have a good chance of winning.

Timber wolves in the Canadian forest testing each other's strength. This sort of play seldom turns into a real fight.

Glossary

barb: a backward-pointing spine that stops a hook, arrow, or quill from being pulled out

bivalve: a mollusk with a shell made of two halves. The halves are hinged so that the shell can open or close. Mussels and clams are bivalves.

camouflage: patterns and colors that help an animal to blend into its background

hind: a female deer, also called a doe

host: a plant or animal on which a parasite lives and from which it obtains food

mimicry: a form of defense in which a species without protection resembles one that is poisonous or has some other defense against predators

mollusk: one of a group of animals that have soft bodies and usually, but not always, hard shells to protect them. Snails, oysters, and octopuses are all mollusks.

parasite: an animal or plant that obtains food and shelter from a larger animal or plant on or in which it lives

predator: any animal that hunts and eats other animals

prey: animals that are hunted and eaten as food by other animals

quill: a long, hollow rod, like the central rod of a feather or the spine of a hedgehog or porcupine

species: a group of animals or plants that have many characteristics in common. Members of one species cannot usually breed with those of another species.

stag: a male deer

territory: an area of land in which an animal or group of animals lives. Animals mark out and protect their territories.

Index

Pages shown in *italic* type include pictures of the animals.

This edition first published 1991 by Lerner Publications Company
Text © 1991 by Jollands Editions
Artwork © 1991 by Cassells Publishers Limited

Library of Congress Cataloging-In-Publication Data
Cherfas, Jeremy.
    Animal defenses / Jeremy Cherfas.
        p.   cm. —(How animals behave)
    Includes index.
    Summary: Describes the wide variety of defenses animals use to protect themselves from predators.
    ISBN 0-8225-2253-5
    1. Animal defenses—Juvenile literature. |1. Animal defenses. 2. Camouflage (Biology)| I. Title. II. Series: Cherfas, Jeremy. How animals behave.
    QL759.C49   1991
    591.57—dc20   90-44255
                                            CIP
                                            AC

Acknowledgments
The publishers wish to thank the following photographers and agencies whose photographs appear in this book. The photographs are credited by page number and position on the page (T-top, B-bottom, L-left, R-right).

Bruce Coleman Ltd.: C. B. and D. W. Frith, 3T; Kim Taylor, 4T, 6, 7T; G. Dore, 7B; Wayne Lankinen, 8T; Bernd Thies, 8B; Jane Burton, 9T; M. P. L. Fogden, 10B, 24TB; Jen and Des Bartlett, 11, 18; Rod Willams, 12T; Carl Roessler, 13, 20T; Gunter Ziesler, 14; Jill Sneesby, 15; Joseph Van Wormer, 17; Bob and Clara Colhoun, 22T; Nevill Coleman, 26B; George McCarthy, 29B; Hans Reinhard, 30; Dennis Green, 27B. Frank Lane Picture Agency Ltd.: Silvestris, 3B; Leonard Lee, 10T; W. S. Clark, 16T; Frank Lane, 20B; L. West, 22; Philip Perry, 25; David Grewcock, 27T; W. Wisniewski, 28B; Terry Whittaker, 29T; Mark Newman, 16B, 28T. Eric and David Hosking: D. P. Wilson, 9B. Nature Photographers Ltd.: S. C. Bisserot, 5B, 26T; Paul Sterry, 5T, 23; Roger Tidman, 12B; James Hyett, 21. Front cover photograph: © Mark F. Wallner

Editorial planning by Jollands Editions
Designed by Alison Anholt-White
Color origination by Golden Cup Printing Co., Ltd, Hong Kong
Printed in Great Britain by Eagle Colourbooks Ltd.

Bound in the United States of America